Creating
Inner
Harmony

ALSO BY DON CAMPBELL

Books

*The Harmony of Health: Sound Relaxation for Mind, Body, and Spirit**

The Mozart Effect®

The Mozart Effect® for Children

100 Ways to Improve Teaching Using Your Voice and Music:
Pathways to Accelerate Learning

Music: Physician for Times to Come

Rhythms of Learning: Creative Tools for Developing Lifelong Skills

The Roar of Silence

Master Teacher, Nadia Boulanger

Introduction to the Musical Brain

The Magic of Amadeus, Volumes 1–7 (Japanese)

Music CDs

Essence

Music for the Mozart Effect, Volumes 1–6 (for Adults)

The Mozart Effect: Music for Babies

The Mozart Effect: Music for Children

The Mozart Effect: Music for Moms & Dads & Moms-to-Be

Spoken Word

The Wisdom and Power of Music

Mozart as Healer

Heal Yourself with Your Own Voice

*Available from Hay House

Please visit Hay House USA: **www.hayhouse.com®**
Hay House Australia: **www.hayhouse.com.au**
Hay House UK: **www.hayhouse.co.uk**
Hay House South Africa: **orders@psdprom.co.za**
Hay House India: **www.hayhouse.co.in**

Creating Inner Harmony

Using Your Voice and Music to Heal

DON CAMPBELL

HAY HOUSE, INC.
Carlsbad, California
London • Sydney • Johannesburg
Vancouver • Hong Kong • New Delhi

Copyright © 2007 by Don Campbell

Published and distributed in the United States by: Hay House, Inc.: www.hayhouse. com • *Published and distributed in Australia by:* Hay House Australia Pty. Ltd.: www. hayhouse.com.au • *Published and distributed in the United Kingdom by:* Hay House UK, Ltd.: www.hayhouse.co.uk • *Published and distributed in the Republic of South Africa by:* Hay House SA (Pty), Ltd.: orders@psdprom.co.za • *Distributed in Canada by:* Raincoast: www.raincoast.com • *Published in India by:* Hay House Publishers India: www.hayhouse.co.in

Editorial supervision: Jill Kramer   •   *Design:* Tricia Breidenthal

Library of Congress Control Number: 2006921970

ISBN: 978-1-4019-0885-0

10 09 08 07   4 3 2 1
1st edition, July 2007

Printed in the United States of America

I dedicate this book to Kevin Townley,
Murray Rogers, Ted Karpf, and John Rosner,
whose ministry to bring harmony to this world
will sing and heal generations to come.

♩ ♪ ♪

Contents

Foreword

The first time I saw Don Campbell weave his magic with sound was in a spare, inhospitable, rented hotel auditorium where he was teaching. The lights were harsh, the seating was uncomfortable, the room was stuffy, and the air was stale. It hardly seemed an environment conducive to learning. But then Campbell stepped forward to teach.

Part muse, part Merlin, he urged his listeners to draw deep and restful breaths. Next he asked them to hum, then to vocalize some simple, elongated vowel sounds. What alchemy was this? The students became alert and focused. The uncomfortable chairs became comfortable enough, and the very air of the room seemed to clear. This was the magic of sound— to soothe, to heal, to integrate, and to inspire.

Before an hour had passed, Don Campbell had his ragtag students sounding like a polished choir. As he led them through the sacred syllables of chant, he wore his scholarship and expertise lightly. A master artist, he had no need for ego. He was instead playful, light, gently reverent, and irreverent. The shyest students opened their voices like Christmas presents. Campbell was encouraging and enticing, both serious and comic as he led his class through a series of ever-deepening exercises.

At the lunch break, Campbell and I repaired to a nearby restaurant. Over salads and tea, he listened to my story. I was 44 years old when music came to me suddenly and inexorably. I heard melody and lyrics simultaneously. I felt an urgency to write what I heard, yet I had no musical training. Campbell listened gravely.

"You don't need to be afraid," he told me. "Sound is healing. What's happening to you is a great gift. Try to trust, and you won't be overwhelmed."

Back in the afternoon session, Campbell emphasized the power of sound to repair the physical self. While he didn't make extravagant claims, it was clear that he believed sound was a healing tool of revolutionary dimensions. It was possible, he felt, to use musical tones to balance the body back into the harmony of health. Gently and patiently, he led his students through some simple experiments, teaching them to sense the resonance of wellness and the dissonance of disease.

"Music has a profound capacity to affect our well-being," Campbell taught. "It can make us more healthy, more vital, more vibrant, and far, far more creative." He led further vocal exercises, showing how to find harmony within. Before the afternoon was half over, the air in the stale room was electric with excitement. These ideas were both simple and profound.

Fifteen years have passed since I met Don Campbell. He's become an internationally famed musical expert following his book *The Mozart Effect.* His seminal ideas have reached hospices, hospitals, universities, and cathedrals. Throughout his increasing acclaim, he has remained modest and playful. The book you hold in your hands reflects the temperament of its author: While its ideas are important, they're never self-important.

As Campbell said on that original afternoon, "Just try these simple tools, and a breakthrough will follow."

— **JULIA CAMERON,**
the author of *The Artist's Way*

And the more souls who resonate together

The greater the intensity of their love

And, mirror-like, each soul reflects the other.

✦✦✦ **DANTE ALIGHIERI** ✦✦✦

In the Beginning

*H*ow many books on music and sound start out with "In the Beginning"? The great universe of sound, the ocean of harmony, the resonant logos, the music of the spheres—it has all been said a thousand times. After 35 years of teaching music, health, and education, I fear the subject has become a cliché. Yet the challenge to write a short book about voice, music, and healing in a creative, fresh manner has been developing in me for years.

After a lifetime in music, I sense that I'm more of a missionary than a performer. I'm now more devoted to the importance of awakening the spirit of music and sound in the listener than to proving anything other than the immense joy, balance, and inspiration that can come to each of us with a slight redesign of our listening skills. Analyzing and attempting to confirm every musical experience with scientific validity is being done by therapists, practitioners, and scientists. Many people believe that just lying back and letting music roll over you is nothing more than "tone bathing," a nice and sometimes relaxing experience.

Yet when we listen and attune our inner voices with music and visual designs, it's possible to enter into a rich reality of conscious balance that can quicken the mind, relax the body, and open multiple venues for creative expression.

A year ago, I wrote *The Harmony of Health,* a visual and musical guide to health and relaxation. Addressing this vast topic in five short, simple exercises and chapters gave me the opportunity to review a lifetime of materials chronicling important discoveries in the mind-body sciences and to develop a new way to harness the power of sound. Now this book—combining powerful visual symbols with music and simple vocal exercises to relax and release the voice—is not only creative, but on the cutting edge for bringing focus, clarity, and well-being to your own personal tool kit.

For nine years, I was director of the Institute for Music, Health, and Education. The subjects I taught focused on toning, the basic vowel sounds of the voice color, and posture. More than 1,000 students participated in the arduous, daily task of making different elongated tones in different postures and documenting how this affected the mind, body, and emotions.

More than 3,000 individuals have participated in my workshops based on toning and sounding the voice. This process, which is overtly simple to do, produces many creative physical and emotional results, and it has led me to write this book.

So, "In the Beginning" is just that. We're beginning to leave the preconceived ideas about your voice, visualization, and creativity for a short time. Working with a chapter a day, you'll explore your voice, inner sounds, and creative ways of awakening . . . and access a powerful new way of self-alignment.

— DON CAMPBELL
Boulder, Colorado

Why — do they shut Me out of Heaven?

Did I sing — too loud?

••• EMILY DICKINSON •••

Chapter 1

Inner Creativity

"*K*eep your voice down!"
"Hush up!"
"Shusssh!"

As children, how many times did we all hear that "silence is golden." When we're sad, the world doesn't want to hear our sighs, cries, and sobs. We feel the pain when others groan and moan; yet the joy of laughter, song, and victorious touchdown chants stays with us and our bodies for a long time.

To understand the very basic nature of our spontaneous responses to the many pangs and delights of life, we must return to the basic utterances of our prehistoric songs and sounds. The core of creativity came from the need to expand our very tonal and simple vocabulary to words, chants, and eventually symphonies. The impetus to find more words, movements, drawings, and other expressive structures has manifested in language, landscape, and athletic performance.

The urge to communicate the necessities of life and emotional feelings starts at birth. The first gasp for air—and the cry of shock at the transition into being initiated into life—exist regardless of what culture or century we live in. Many societies have songs and myths of creation that include breath and sound.

Language—no matter how primitive and essential—is a combination of tones, rhythms, and inflections that determine the framework of a culture. Whether it evolves into poetry, oratorios, screenplays, or popular songs, the tone is there—primal and similar in all parts of the world.

This book is about the creative exploration back to the source of your expression and first utterance. The sounds, music, and visualizations at the end of each chapter aren't simply a journey backward, but a powerhouse of creative and healing experience that can connect you to the deep well of understanding that dwells in your preverbal center. This book is a guide to using your inner, expressive voice for bringing balance and health to your mind and body.

In my last book, *The Harmony of Health,* I presented an easy and effective way to relax and refresh the mind and body with beautiful music and images of a heart, circle, triangle, crescent, and star. To begin a creative inner journey, the ability to release tension and relax is paramount.

Each of the five chapters in this book includes sounding exercises that are both auditory and silent. Learning to "think" a tone is an effective and immediate way to help bring clarity to the mind. Also, each chapter has a powerful and dynamic image with a symbol in the center to focus the eyes and give a visual aid. This helps keep the mind and voice in a stable place for the creative journey within.

The CD that accompanies this book has five wonderful pieces of music that allow the inner voice to relax and refresh the mind. The vocal tonal image, the visual picture, and the music move in concert to inspire this exploration. There's no need to be a singer, an artist, or a meditator; you can still easily use these tools to improve your state of concentration, creativity, and relaxation.

The Edge of Creativity

After 30 years of writing and reading about the process of creativity, I'm still challenged to define it. For a decade, I've been convinced that it consists of the moments "on the edge," whether it's a child exploring with blocks in a crib, my mother attempting a new recipe, or jazz musicians stretching their improvisational skills. The edge changes and adapts with age, experience, and talent; and it has a reality of tension, newness, and exploration within it. This can come from challenges, pains, and deep inner quests, as well as transformation, beauty, and intimacy. *The edge has energy rather than being just a passive state.*

To have a new idea when the light goes off in our heads may be the foundation of creativity, but that alone isn't enough to manifest a process. In Mihaly Csikszentmihalyi's popular book *Flow: The Psychology of Optimal Experience,* he explores the scientific and emotional processes that bring us into a state of productivity and experimentation. This leads to absolute absorption in the moment and the experience. The ability to be focused as a listener, performer, or meditator can be reached through movement, breath, concentration, or that simple flash of enjoyment that suddenly awakens us to a state of well-being.

Creativity, I sense, is dual in nature. One part of the process is to set up the experience with the environment and necessary tools, while the other part is one of improvisation, flow, and dancing with the edge of perception. I wish there were a formula—for the jazz player, high school poet, amateur actor, and orchestral conductor—since all of them have vastly different responsibilities to themselves and their public.

Some creativity is exquisitely private and other forms seem to be for public consumption. Lorin Hollander, master concert pianist and former child prodigy, describes in his workshops and lectures how he entered states of creative expression and almost ecstasy when spending hours at the piano, yet experienced pure terror when he was being judged by his teachers. Beethoven felt the agony of genius and creativity by writing and rewriting his compositions over and over from a place of stress, while Mozart just looked for the time to jot down the music that was cosmically, intuitively flowing through him.

Who's the most creative: the one who's in a state of stress and agony, or the one in ecstasy and pleasure? There's no answer except the observation that we can all enter into a creative flow from wherever we are. The ability to develop this inner skill when there's no one looking on or judging is a rich source for our life, whether we feel talented or not.

How we are wired, connected, and nurtured through the senses produces the tools through which our logic and words (left brain), spatial and abstract

ability to observe (right brain), and emotions and feelings (limbic system) make up our creative potential.

In my 1983 book *Introduction to the Musical Brain,*
I took an absolutely creative approach to this topic. It
pushes the reader to the edge of logic with drawings,
musical exercises, and humor; it volleys and thun-
ders right into the arena of original ways to think
and be with music education. My wild and youthful
approaches to teaching and writing have served an
important purpose as resources for some of the available patterns of thinking, feeling, and actions in the
brain that create new pathways for expression.

Now, 17 books later, with translations into 22 languages, I must admit that there are so many opportu-
nities for growth and creativity that are influenced by
the age, experience, and environment of each individual. Each spring the University of Colorado brings
hundreds of creative minds into a wild think tank
called the Conference on World Affairs. Panels flour-
ish on every political, social, religious, and artistic
topic, as great minds and artists are meshed together in groups where one topic is discussed from the

perspective of multiple disciplines. (Past topics include: Any Good Religions Out There?, Science for Dummies, and Philosophies of Peace and War. See **www.colorado.edu/cwa** for more information.) For the past 58 years, Nobel laureates, first ladies, wild jazz musicians, political activists, and great writers have been undoing the minds of thousands of listeners. The form is conservative, and the outcome is often genius.

Ho-hum or Humdinger?

As we developed as children, we needed color, movement, light, and other kinds of stimulation that gave us ingredients to provide a foundation for our neural and physical growth. Creativity grew from these vital components. Yet years later, we can often find ourselves so overstimulated that we're numb. Hypersensitive kids often can't concentrate on any one thing for long periods of time, and my book

Introduction to the Musical Brain left out a major and very important component for creativity: quiet.

In a way, this is like digestion. We must have time to let our bodies assimilate the nutrients and discard the unneeded components of food. We think that naps and sleep states do this for us, and that's true. Yet *conscious* downtime, relaxed awakening, and very focused quiet periods may be the factors forgotten by our overfed world of media.

Inner creativity may seem to some like a state of meditation or contemplation, but it doesn't always need to happen in an unmoving state. It can occur while walking, raking leaves, cooking, or just enjoying nature. And rather than being quiet and passive in this book, we'll be using the voice as a gateway to the alignment of mind, body, and spirit. This serves to release tension and unresolved emotions, soothing the mind and simultaneously producing a deeper and more balanced breathing pattern.

Our work with the voice isn't about speaking or singing. Through "toning," we'll develop a tool that can be a significant guide through times of stress or pain. It also opens a variety of ways to be more creative, aware, and focused. This technique prolongs the vowel sounds in a relaxed way. It's a tool that guides us into the balanced, awakened state of focus.

Along with our voices, we'll use an image (for visual focus) and wonderful music. This isn't complicated, just a simple way to align our senses of listening, looking, and sounding.

The goal of this little book isn't to create either boredom or sensorial exuberance. Instead, its purpose is to go within, entering the forums of our own mind and creating clean and fresh pathways to harmony and resonant attention. By releasing the endless thoughts and possibilities that stimulate us, we'll use tools of visualization, music, and our own inner voices in order to sense an abundance of internal wealth. This may be a form of creativity completely new to you, so just enjoy the simplicity and process. Give yourself five days—or five weeks, if you feel the need—to explore each of these small chapters.

Using Voice, Music, Visualization, and Affirmations for This Chapter

Step One

The beginning is about the *hum,* the gentle soft utterance within the throat. The lips are closed, the jaw is relaxed, and the exhalation is making a soft sigh. At first it may be a short, easy release with a lot of air; then it may become a simple and slight expression of pleasure. The goal is to naturally release the humming sound, not to hum a tune or make it necessarily audible to anyone other than yourself.

Take three or four minutes to sit comfortably, release your breath, and just *hum.*

Affirmation:
HUMmmmmmmmmmmmm . . . I rest in the sound.

Take a few minutes to feel the affirmation . . .
then close your eyes and whisper it to yourself . . .
and then think it silently.

Step Two

After the affirmation feels comfortable and spontaneous, look at the design on page 17. This stable
and concrete portal holds a simple white line in its
center. Follow this process:

- Look at the image for a few minutes without
  blinking. Sit up with the book directly in front
  of you so that your head isn't tilting down.

- Notice your breath and how the energy in
  the design may change during your slow
  breathing.

- Now begin to *hum* as you gaze into this form.

- Then add the affirmation for a few minutes:
  HUMMMMMMMMMMMMM . . . I rest in the sound.

- Close your eyes, gently sit in quiet, and feel
  the effects of the exercise.

Step Three

Play Track 1 of the CD. This is a piece called "Piano Concerto No. 5 in E Major," by J. S. Bach.

- Look at the figure.

- Begin the music.

- Think the *humming* sound, feeling its energy
  as you look and listen.

- When Track 1 finishes, turn off the CD and
  sit with your eyes closed. Notice the inner
  sense of balance.

This basic system will be used throughout the book: becoming aware of the sound of your voice, using the affirmation, focusing your awareness on the visual form, and listening to music. This multi-sensorial recipe will lead you to many wonderful moments.

Do this first exercise a number of times. You may wish to journal your experiences on the pages following the image and allow your poetic powers to be expressed; you may want to draw, improvise at the piano, or just meditate. All is well and appropriate.

HUMmmmmmmmmmmm . . .
I rest in the sound.

Music: Track 1
J. S. Bach, "Piano Concerto No. 5 in E Major, BWV 1056
- Largo"; Hae-won Chang, piano; Camerata Cassovia; Róbert
Stankovsky, conductor; 2:46

What I observe about my breath:

_____

_____

_____

_____

What I feel from the music:

_____

_____

_____

_____

_____

What I notice with the *hum* sound:

_____

_____

_____

_____

_____

What I sense from the image with tone:

_____

_____

_____

_____

_____

Tune the music of your life's melody to carefree, harmless notes, and thus, through your innate nature, become Divine.

••• **THE VEDAS** •••

Chapter 2

The Breath of Tone and Harmony

Ah, to breathe. Years ago, I was listening to Louise Shrader, a perky octogenarian in the northern suburbs of Dallas. She was telling me that the most boring thing in the afterlife was the inability to breathe.

"You can think, move, travel, and not worry about the body, but you just don't have any way to inhale or exhale. I just love to smell and breathe—they're the best parts of life."

This seemed like an odd statement from a devout Methodist woman. Where did she get her knowledge or intuition?

Louise's ideas came to mind last winter when I was unable to breathe through my nose because of an acute allergy that closed my nasal passages. Nights of restless sleep and days of experimentation with acupuncture, natural, and traditional medicine put me in a state of deep frustration. It was an effort to take a simple, natural inhalation. Months of meditation and visualization had helped, but I longed to just inhale without any effort.

After consulting medical experts on allergies and the nose, I discovered I had inflammations and a deviated septum caused by a broken nose I incurred as a child. After a medical procedure, I was able to sleep and feel refreshed. I now awaken each morning with a consummate appreciation for the energy that's available through the air around us.

Yoga has always emphasized the importance of understanding the deeper experience of breath and *prana,* the life force. What seems to be somewhat mystical and foreign to the Western mind is obvious and fundamental in the philosophies of China, India, and most of the rest of Asia. Spirit and breath have been interchangeable in many languages. For example, the word *ruach* in the first chapter of Genesis indicates clearly that the "breath" or "spirit" of God hovered over the waters. Life was created and continues to be sustained by the impulse to breathe.

In this chapter, becoming conscious of breath as the core of nature and creativity is the goal. Something so automatic and natural seems obvious, yet becoming aware of inhalation and exhalation in our working, exercising, thinking, and sleeping can give us a very powerful tool to help us relax and focus. The purpose is to "inspire" us.

"I Am Inspiration," an Exercise

- Sit back with ease in a comfortable chair so that you have a feeling of lightness. Relax, close your eyes, and imagine your body as a balloon. While inhaling, sense your body expanding with natural ease. Then while exhaling, visualize your body releasing air from the pores of your skin.

- You may start by focusing on your feet and legs for a few breaths, then add the flow in and out of your torso. Continue upward to your shoulders, arms, and hands. Then as you inhale and inspire, bring air into all parts of your body. You may sense the oxygenation of your blood sending life and calm energy to the cells of your body.

- For a few minutes, continue to sense the "balloon" expanding and releasing with slow and easy breaths.

- When you feel relaxed, begin a *humming* sound with a loose jaw for a couple of breaths, and then allow an *"ah"* sound to begin on the exhalation. Drop your jaw ever so gently and notice when the sound begins and ends. There's no need to force it . . . just slowly begin and release.

- Let your critical and verbal mind go with each breath, and fill the imaginary balloon of your body with lightness. Release it slowly with the *ah,* which may be a whisper more than a vocalized sound. This is the quiet presence of breath.

Toning

There's a remarkable amount of sound within the physical body, since not only the breath and heartbeat contain musical properties. The pulse of blood flowing and the billions of rhythmic dances among the brain cells all create a vast orchestration far beyond our auditory range. Silent and still moments are filled with a subtle transmission of movement, with the occasional fireworks of digestion. If we actually heard the precise, nonstop pattern within these systems, we wouldn't be able to focus on the outer world.

Exploring our own vibratory awareness is more than just being still and calm; it's often filled with a heightened awareness of the elemental breath. So many times in meditation, we just think of the inhalation and exhalation, but here we'll begin to listen to energy with the aid of visual and auditory tools.

As we progress through this book, we'll experience the creative power of the simplest sounds we can make. From *humming* to yawning, the *ahhhh, oooou*, and *eeeee* all have very interesting effects on the mind and body. These basic tones hold the emotions we know as pain and pleasure, and the vibration of the breath is the basic urge to vocalize. Whether we cry or coo, moan or sigh, we release feelings through our body. We automatically soothe ourselves, even though it may irritate those around us. As infants and children, these are the tools that let the world know we're here!

Toning is the elongation of vowels. It can be audible yet quiet, loud and strident, or even silent and mental. This process involves holding on to the sound inwardly and outwardly and allowing the breath to release and energize the mind and body.

Think of it as the imprint of energy upon the exhaled breath. If the sound is a calm *ah*, it might have the form of gentle waves:

If the sound is a highly charged *eeeee*, it may have a form similar to this:

The image may not seem calming, but the contrast created in relation to the *ah* sound demonstrates how powerful the toning voice can be.

More than 30 years ago, I became aware of the power of tonality in movement. Great teachers of movement and music—such as Rudolf Steiner, Émile Jacques-Dalcroze, Rudolf Von Laban, Martha Stockton, F. M. Alexander, Margaret Allen, and Charlotte Selver—emphasized the indigenous tonal power of gesture, motion, and rhythmic movement. It's a challenge to articulate the subtleties of this inner world expressed in movement and sound; words truly can't describe the experience of music or movement. These remarkable teachers were able to slow down both the mental and physical perceptions and sensations to analyze the source of energy that underlies the expressive impulse. In a way, they all sensed it as an inaudible tone.

Often as children we feel such a harmonic flow when we hear music that we begin to move and sway. Throughout our lives, we continue to find our feet tapping along with the beat of a great song. I'll never forget the time I was playing the piano for my mother and the residents of the Alzheimer's and dementia unit of a nursing home in Austin, Texas. When I began to play and sing one of my mom's favorite pieces, "Ain't She Sweet, as She's Walkin' Down the Street," everyone began to clap and smile. A woman named Mabel, who normally didn't move, speak, or smile, suddenly began to tap her right foot perfectly to the beat. When the music connected her brain to her body, she became involved with this outer world.

Kids so often love singing and playing instruments until they need to translate written notes into sound. Then they may think that they aren't meant to be involved in this art because they can't read music. In researching this, Martha Stockton discovered early in the 20th century that there's an "inner pulse," a breathing center that's the core of the moving musical experience. After studies in Europe, she began to teach Creative Motion throughout the United States. It was one of the first American mind-body-spirit techniques that used the whole being to enter into a state of flow and resonance with music. She was certain that tension kept people from entering into this place of balance in the listening or performance mode.

Thousands of teachers and students throughout the world have integrated movement, breath, and music together. The tone underneath sound, the tonal center, and the core of energy . . . all have sought ways to identify with this balanced place of power. As we begin to integrate the breath with the voice, using both visual and musical tools, you may be able to sense it. Tai chi, yoga, tae kwon do, and many of the movement arts speak of the solar plexus as the center of the energy that can be sourced by gesture, movement, and breath.

I personally think that there are 100 or more different ways to reach this place of centering and prolong the state of awareness. The longer it's experienced (the tone, place of resonant flow), the more inner wisdom we have about a world that's always available. To use it daily is to build a creative internal resource for that sense of connection with our spirit. It then begins to reflect in the world around us in both word and action.

Many people discover that place of inner awareness through prayer or meditation, and it then extends toward an active conscious place where normal, habitual activities are awakened. This quiet place of activity is powerful and energized, not passive or sleepy. Buddhism speaks of it, and Thomas Keating writes of the active power of Centering Prayer. Often I refer to the "IT place," "the real I," or my soul place.

♪

WHO is the   I that remembers joy and peace?
I that feels pain and knows it will pass?
I that creates and releases?
I that observes this world and the future?
I that prays, doubts, and loves?
I that forgets and yet knows?

WHO is tone, the soul, the point
around which the spirit dances
that knows no time, knows all
space, and connects everything.
There's no question.

♪

Moving from the more abstract and philosophical thoughts, we can begin the simple and most enjoyable ways to listen and make sounds. Bobby McFerrin is a vocal genius of our time. He can form virtual landscapes, oceans, and clouds with his voice. From classical scores, which he calls "paper music," to instantaneous improvisation, he's found dozens of languages within the scope and tone of the voice. Whether he's conducting a symphonic ensemble or a group of volunteer improv singers from an audience, he simply dances with his voice. His body makes the music.

So whether you're a singer inside or outside the shower, the following exercise is really about another kind of energy: elongating the tone and letting the sound massage your body from the inside out. Let the vibration do the work. The more you relax, listen, and flow with the vowel sound, the more rewards you'll receive.

Using Voice, Music, Visualization, and Affirmations for This Chapter

Step One

Aaah is the most relaxing of all sounds. You can make it with just your breath before there's any kind of vocalization. The lips are open, the jaw is relaxed, and the exhalation makes a soft sigh. It is the beginning of a yawn.

Take three or four minutes to enjoy the sound of *ah* and the exhaled breath.

Affirmation:
AAAAAH . . . the joy of breath.

Take a few minutes to feel the affirmation . . . then close your eyes and whisper it to yourself . . . then think it silently.

Step Two

After the affirmation feels comfortable and spontaneous, look at the design on page 39. This stable and concrete gateway to peace holds an infinity sign in its center. There's no need to be intimidated by the structure of strong portals; they only look ominous when you aren't relaxed. You may want to imagine that this is just an entrance to a huge and safe space, where there's openness, clarity, and fresh air.

- Look at the image for a few minutes without blinking. Sit up with the book directly in front of you so that your head isn't tilting down.

- Become aware of the gentle flowing form of the infinity sign.

- Notice your breath and how the energy in the design may change during your slow breathing. You may wish to let your eyes follow the shape as you breathe. I typically inhale while visually tracing three loops and exhale for three loops.

- Next, begin to vocalize your exhaling voice as you gaze into this form.

- Then add the affirmation for a few minutes: *AAAAAH . . . the joy of breath.*

- Close your eyes, gently sit in quiet, and feel the effects of the exercise.

Step Three

Play Track 2 of the enclosed CD. This familiar piece, "Gymnopédie No. I," by Eric Satie, has a breathing pattern of its own. Is it comfortable for you to enter the breath of the music?

- Look at the figure.

- Begin the music.

- Think the *AAAAAH* sound, feeling its energy as you look and listen.

- When Track 2 finishes, turn off the CD and sit with your eyes closed, noticing the inner sense of balance.

Become aware of the sound of your voice, the affirmation, your focused awareness of the visual form, and the music. This multisensorial recipe leads us to many wonderful moments.

Do this exercise a number of times. You may wish to journal your experiences and allow your poetic powers to be expressed. You might want to draw, improvise at the piano, or just meditate. All is well and appropriate.

AAAAAH . . .
the joy of breath!

Music: Track 2
Satie, "Gymnopédie No. I," Gerald Garcia, guitar; CSFR State
Philharmonic Orchestra (Kosice); Peter Breiner, conductor; 2:59

What I observe about my breath:

_____

_____

_____

_____

What I feel from the music:

_____

_____

_____

_____

What I notice with the *AAAAAH* sound:

What I sense from the image with tone:

Music is the
voice of all sorrow,
all joy. It needs
no translation.

••• **HELEN EXLEY** •••

Chapter 3

Your Inner Voice

Life's rhythms and tones modify throughout the day with routine movement, interactions, and exercise. After we eat or sleep, we have quite a different balancing symphony playing throughout our body than we did earlier. Where there is outer stimulation, it's more difficult to sense the ongoing energetic flow. Our deep inner voice is often hidden by all the stimulation of daily life, and we also learn to use our thoughts to cover it.

Learning to access this place of rich nourishment—often called the "small, still voice of God"—can be a long-term affair. After exercising, or prolonged periods of toning or chanting, this internal world can awaken and give us remarkable wisdom and energy for our daily routines.

There's a tone for every emotion. From the spontaneous response to a winning touchdown to the moments of irritation when we have to wait in a long line, a wealth of ongoing energies are continually at work. Whether the source is tormenting thunder or haunting quiet, we exist in a state of tone. When we're in a smooth, relaxed mood with no agitation, the vibration is constant and part of the mild, almost unnoticed *aaaah* state. Feelings are a continual melody in the mind and body—in fact, sometimes this "tune" continues as we sleep and underlies the pains and joys of each day.

Even a momentary moan or laugh sends energy to our neck, head, and upper torso. The vibration actually massages us from the inside out. While speaking, we're sending frequencies throughout the bones in the skull. By elongating a vowel, we can actually feel an epicenter of the vibration. When talking rapidly, there's little time for the energy to localize, yet there *is* a tonal center in our normal speaking voices. It's regarded as high or low, rich or shallow. The timbre changes with our moods, sometimes reflecting a lifeless sound or a roaring rage.

Actually, the intonation and inflection of our voices often can project more information than the words we use. Let's take a phrase and play with it for a few minutes. Where the words or syllables are italicized, prolong the sounds—stretch them more than you would normally.

I feel all right.

I feel *allll* right.

I *feeeel* all right.

Each of these examples gives a slightly different meaning to the phrase. Experiment now with the following sentences and see how many different moods you can create by varying the rhythm and tone. End each phrase with a higher sound, then a lower one. Imagine a question mark or an exclamation point at the end of the line. Stress some of the syllables and then make some of them short and disjointed.

- Right, that sounds creative to me.
- Of course, I love to spend hours cooking.
- About $100—that's the price.
- That's an interesting smell.

Intrigue, judgment, excitement, boredom, curiosity, and empowerment can all come from our tones of voice. Beneath our words lies the impulse to speak and relate to the world around us. So as we use a different vowel sound in each of these chapters, we can realize that every utterance has a wide range of powers. There are a thousand variants in each voice. By allowing ourselves to listen and feel the sensations, we easily realize that we can tune spirits and bodies as musicians tune their instruments.

My Tone, My Being

Toning is as old as chant, prayer, and the beginnings of language. Eastern chants used the *om* mantra or sound to bring focus to the mind and body; it releases thoughts and brings us to a state of meditation. In the early church, chants were assigned tones as centers or modes of a simple phrase. In 1711, Jonathan Swift wrote of "tuning and toning each Word, each Syllable and Letter to their due Cadence," as a necessary practice to know the deepest experience of inner and outer meaning.

All of us can do amazing things by simply adjusting the tone of our inner voices. The practices of being conscious, aware, and "real" all point to this ability to integrate the outer world with our inner tone. Often great trauma in childhood creates an underlying tension, fear, and even psychosis. Unexpressed grief and pain can be held within the body as well.

In the nine years that I directed the Institute for Music, Health, and Education, I could sometimes hear blockages in the toning voice of my students. The elongated sound often gave obvious indications of their physical and mental well-being. When I heard a slow, natural glissando—that is, a slide from the higher to the lower parts of a voice on an *ah* or *eeee* sound—it was easy to detect what was strained in the mind/body connection.

You don't need a trained singing voice to make these sounds because toning is the natural spontaneous imprint of a vowel on the breath. Bigger gestures by the body, as well as slight movements of the hands and head, all make interesting changes in the tone. When vocal sound becomes automatic in speech or song, we lose the mind/body connection, yet I wouldn't suggest that we should be in a state of deep awareness at all times. Our ritual habits such as eating, driving, working, and speaking usually have healthy patterns. They can, however, become so routine over time that inner connections and creativity end up smothered by the outer world.

For relaxation and energetic stimulation, tone is an easy gateway to a more integrated self. Finding it is a perpetual process, however, because we're a wealth of vibrating variation. The tones of our bodies change throughout our lives because of age, health, and genetics; and our mental states determine their "color"—for example, if we're in a happy and healthy phase of life, it's brighter. A clarinet and flute may play the same pitch, but have very different personalities, and the same is true for different people. Great choirs learn to blend the individual sounds to become one great voice, yet each member has his or her own personality when speaking or singing independently.

The spontaneous tone, prolonged and uninhibited, has the power to release the temporary and long-held tensions in our body. Toning for eight to ten minutes a day in a variety of postures can provide a more balanced and healthy engagement with your environment as words and thoughts become less rushed and more integrated. The simplicity allows you to experiment and notice how the harmony of your inner and outer worlds begins to blend.

Pitching Out the Pain

Betty Brenneman, a musician and teacher in Racine, Wisconsin, studied toning with me for a year. We became good friends, having both studied music in France. One day as she walked to work, she slipped on the ice and broke her ankle. Within 20 seconds or so, she intuitively went through the vowel sounds and found that *oooooh* quickly removed all discomfort. When she stopped sounding, the pain returned, so she tuned in to the tone once again and it left. During her healing process, she toned often and visualized the healing of her ankle. It mended quickly, and still, many years later, she is pain free.

Children cry with pain, and if we could direct that energy of both fear and anguish into a power of release and health, their discomfort would be greatly modified. I don't mean to imply that tone is a miracle, but it can serve us well to breathe deeply, release emotional stress, and divert our own attention from a shock- and fear-based experience.

The dentist's chair is a good place to begin experimenting with your own inner sounds. It's neither polite nor feasible to make a high *eeee* sound when the drill begins, but you can hum and match that high pitch in your mind. It's amazing to see how many children are able to release their fear by just thinking of Old MacDonald's *"eee-I-eee-I-oooooh"* during a visit to the dentist, and it's possible for you to rehearse for your next appointment, too. Imagine making the high *eeee* sound and relax your jaw. Do this a few times and notice the difference in your own mental well-being.

I've heard hundreds of stories about pain, melody, and tone. The voice is much more powerful than simply listening to music. For example, some compositions that help calm us may actually increase pain. Sometimes we need sounds that block the sensation, while at other times we need to relax and let the suffering gradually be released. Whether it's for chronic back pain *(oooooooow)*, headaches *(eeeeeeeh)* or just an itch *(eeee)*, there's an inner energy within each sound. Search for this, relax into it, and breathe.

For more details on toning, read my book *The Roar of Silence*. The audio version allows the listener to hear the sounds of the tones. My CD *Heal Yourself with Your Own Voice* also offers many exercises for your exploration.

A Still, Small Voice

As we continue to journey inward and open the awareness of the "still, small voice" within, there's the haunting fear that some people have about their vocal capabilities being too limited—too quiet or soft. I've worked with many airy and whispering voices and often find that for these people, the energy of loud, imposing speech or singing is overwhelming. This is either caused by hypersensitive hearing or a childhood where there was auditory abuse, such as with loud music.

Rest assured, the goal here isn't to be either loud or operatic; the purpose is to actually feel the energy of the vowel-imprinted vocal sound upon the body. A light *hum* may be just as powerful as a loud *eeeek*. The powerful exercises at the end of each chapter assist you in keeping a focused, elongated sound while you're listening to the music or looking at the center of the image.

The intention is to allow the tone you make or think to harmonize with your consciousness. In just a few weeks, you'll naturally find creative ways to redesign that internal world with your inner voice. The multiple steps of listening, looking, and toning have one goal: to integrate awareness into a place of awakened balance, energy, and relaxation.

Using Voice, Music, Visualization, and Affirmations for This Chapter

Step One

The awakened sound of the word *day* is filled with brightness and energy. Whether you think of it as the utterance *eh* or a flowing *way,* the sound is made with an open mouth. *Eh* can be a question mark or a laugh. It isn't passive; there's an inner light within the sound of the word itself. Relax the jaw and feel the invigoration of the positive *eh* for a couple of minutes. Close your eyes and feel the energy of the sound in the middle of your head, just between your eyes. You won't fall asleep with this one.

Now begin to speak the affirmation. Enjoy the sensations of speaking the words aloud.

Affirmation:
AAAAY . . . the joy of the inner way.

Take a few minutes to feel the affirmation . . . then close your eyes and whisper it to yourself . . . then think it silently.

Step Two

After the affirmation feels comfortable and spontaneous, look at the design on page 59. This stable and concrete portal holds a simple vertical, elongated diamond in its center. There's no need to be intimidated by the structure of this strong portal. It only looks ominous when you aren't relaxed. You may want to imagine that the gateway and the diamond are just an entrance to a huge and safe space where there's openness, clarity, and fresh air.

- Look at the image for a few minutes without blinking. Sit up with the book directly in front of you so that your head isn't tilting down.

- Become aware of the gentle flowing form of the simple "stretched" diamond.

- Notice your breath and how the energy in the design may change with your slow rhythm. You may wish to let your eyes follow the shape of the form as you breathe. I visualize inhaling into the center of the diamond and filling its bottom and top simultaneously. Then I exhale slowly from the center.

- Now begin to vocalize your exhaling voice as you gaze into this form.

- Then for a few minutes add the affirmation *AAAAY . . . the joy of the inner way.*

- Close your eyes, gently sit in quiet, and feel the effects of the exercise.

Step Three

Play Track 3 of the enclosed CD. The beauty of the well-known Paganini melody is passionate and powerful. (Rachmaninoff created the famous piano variations from this tune.) This arrangement for violin and piano has the brightness of day, the beauty of nature, and the joy of emotion.

- Look at the figure and imagine walking into the diamond, into a beautiful place where it's fresh and cool.

- Begin the music.

- Think the *AAAAY* sound, feeling its energy as you look and listen.

- When Track 3 finishes, turn off the CD and sit with your eyes closed and let your inner voice rest. Be quiet and allow the body and mind to balance.

AAAAY . . .
the joy of the inner way.

Music: Track 3
Rachmaninoff, "Eighteenth Variation," (from "Rhapsody
on a Theme by Paganini," Op. 43, arranged by F. Kreisler);
Takako Nishizaki, violin; Jenö Jandó, piano; 2:55

Observations on the breath:

_____

_____

_____

_____

_____

Feeling from the music:

_____

_____

_____

_____

_____

What I notice with the *AAAAY* sound:

_____

_____

_____

_____

What I sense from the image with tone:

_____

_____

_____

_____

_____

Some kinds of music dissipate in seconds. Other kinds remain a lifetime, Stored in the limbs, in the brain, Or even the heart.

••• DERRICK DE KERCKHOVE •••

Chapter 4

The Sound of Balance

There's an energetic map in the human body. In what seemed like wishful thinking a few decades ago, we can now look into the energy of the brain and the rest of the physical body. By using electromagnetic currents, the magnetic resonance imaging (MRI) machine can realign the polarity of the cells in the body so that it can be photographed. From ultrasonic views of the unborn to CAT and PET scans, we can gaze at the mysterious energetic byways of life.

From the cycles of neural synapses to the rhythmic dance of the limbs and muscles throughout the body, medical science is able to probe into our depths. The energies and "hot spots" of the body are used in Chinese and Indian medicine. The mystical rumors about Eastern energies are becoming a more measured reality each year. What we think and how we use our imagination actually can modify and sometimes control these power centers.

New experiments in sonic acupuncture and tuning-fork body alignment are always interesting to me. A wealth of adventures in my field by intuitives is matched by the clinical explorations of music therapists and medical researchers. Although they may be centuries apart in techniques, these practitioners are forever pushing at the boundaries between intuition and science.

What may seem subtle and mystical to a Western sound practitioner may be simply obvious and sacred to a Chinese or Nepalese shaman. Likewise, if we're deeply spiritual and intuitive, it may be difficult to understand the clinical procedures of music therapy.

Academically trained practitioners or therapists may find it hard to see how the religious and nonmaterial traditions can have credibility.

Pat Moffitt Cook, Ph.D., director of the Open Ear Center on Bainbridge Island, Washington, writes:

> In moments where life forces wane and fears take hold, patients reach for culturally conditioned deep-seated psycho-social and spiritual beliefs for comfort and healing. Musical healers from world cultures harness the emotional and psychic energies of their patients through prescribed songs, rhythms and other musical elements known to positively affect ensuing mental pathologies. These sonic interventions require both the clinical and intuitive skills of sound and music therapists who frequently find themselves traversing the realms of science and spirituality, causing them to work in concert.

Tone Is More Than Sound

The term *tone* is relatively new in the mind-body field, when associated with the voice. The word was used in ancient music to designate the beginning of a scale or the centering note in a piece of music; it also describes the color or pitch of a sound. Laurel Elizabeth Keyes of Denver, Colorado, began to use the term in the 1950s to describe the subtle and yet powerful energy inside the vocal utterance.

When I met her, I was taken by the most intimate and pleasing way she made sounds. It was quite different from what I'd learned in my musical studies, holding a power that was not controlled like a great singer. It was, she said, "an energy inside the sound." My musical brain was stunned. She helped me start a daily practice that evolved into a dramatic release of energy in 1981 when I spent nearly a day and a half in a state of tone. (I describe this in detail in my book *The Roar of Silence*.)

The word *tone* is used with great insight in a clinical context. When a doctor asks you to flex or stretch a limb or muscle, the resistance is called tone; a decrease in this quality is called "hypotonia." When the lack of tone makes us weak, our muscles might feel floppy or we may collapse like rag dolls.

Silvia Nakkach, music therapist and director of the Vox Mundi Project in San Francisco, has taken the performance styles of India, the Americas, and Europe to a new height in her vocal teaching. She writes:

> The voice as a fabric of breath, tone and expression has the capacity to convey and release emotions like no other instrument. [It's capable] of microtonal intervals [and] divisions of semi-tones. . . . [This quality gives us] the capacity to expand the senses and proves to be naturally entrancing, reaffirming the intimacy in the therapeutic relationship. It also creates a sense of 'journeying,' while allowing enough time to connect with the emotion that needs to be released.

Nakkach observed that "pre-melodic vocal practices" were quite differentiated from melody-based chanting. The ancient forms facilitate deep listening while also relaxing the body and the mind, and improving physiological functioning. This type of sounding and toning also provides a valuable means of inducing a contemplative and sacred atmosphere.

Both Pat Cook at the Open Ear Center and Silvia Nakkach at the Vox Mundi Project have developed schools devoted to understanding how indigenous cultures can make significant contributions to the way we use the arts in modern therapy and health care. Janis Page, a sound practitioner, finds both of these programs brilliant in the way they take the roots and lineage of sound healing into practical realms. She has said, "By constantly listening for the container of the transformational energy in the form of tone, drone, or rhythm, I can understand and experience how sound has so much power. We can pass the lineage forward to the next generation with both wisdom and understanding."

To learn more about these schools, refer to the Suggested Reading section at the end of this book.

Ring Tone, Tummy Tone, Muscle Tone, Dermatone, and Tonettes

I remember playing a small, flutelike plastic instrument called a "tonette" when I was young; it was a tuned, whistling flute. When I was in the fourth grade, it was noisy and squeaky—even deafening—when it was blown too hard. When the breath was gentle and controlled, however, it had a sweet sound. Later, in music school, I learned that *tone* could be controlled for beauty and creative expression. Today I see the word on television in advertisements of every kind—for mobile phones, a weight-loss program, and the creation of perfect skin. There are even claims that there are tones for cells in the body to make them ring and resonate so that they're in balance and bring health to the body.

Whether we interpret the term as being musical or vibrational with symbolic meaning, exploring the body's energy centers through sound is a fascinating journey. As we learn to perceive the relationship of objective vowels and interpreted resonating energy, we can learn to "listen" to ourselves in a much more refined manner. From meridians to chakras, maps of the body enrich our understanding of the broad spectrum of ambient energies and emotions within us. The simple act of toning heightens our awareness of our own inner power and vibrations. Through that consciousness, we feel more alive and connected with everything around us.

Intuitive toning is a wonderful way to develop an inner vocabulary for energy, release, and centering. Every individual actually creates different flavors of sound. A person's speaking voice may be light and airy, yet he or she can sing with force, while a rich speaking voice may turn breathy while singing. The range—how high and low a pitch is produced—is different in the speaking, singing, and toning.

A tone in the high register has a very different energy in the low register. Your daily health, posture, and emotional state produce inflections in the voice in the most personal of ways. Thus, it's difficult to provide a menu of what tones are best for you. In each of the exercises in this book, we're concentrating on the inner sound—the thought of it, and how to focus it in the mind.

♪

To help you get more comfortable with the outer sounds, I've included a simple exploration list (on page 73) to allow your intuition to flow with sounds.

It takes two or three minutes for the brain and the physical body to respond to the breath and vibration. Although you may feel instant stimulation with the EE sound, make it calmly and smoothly.

In advanced work, there's exploration of the postures and visual focus. In the beginning, there's no need to tone for more than 12 or 15 minutes. Let go of all expectations; allow the experience to come to you without too much thought. Toning, in the truest sense, is about the whole body, not specifically the voice. It's like a lightbulb that brings awareness to a whole room. *There is no need to look directly into the light of tone; just be aware of the interior space without judgment, evaluation, or criticism.* Sometimes four minutes of sounding then resting or meditating for another four minutes before beginning again gives an impressive and memorable sense of the power of tone.

Tones for Harmony

Use these elongated tones to help you tune in to your consciousness.

Use relaxed sounds that are not strained or too high in pitch.

AH – relaxation, calm release, peace

EH – awakening, brightening consciousness

EE – stimulation, sudden awareness

OU – physical peace, spaciousness

OO – fullness, integration, spiritual awareness

MM – balancing, restfulness

♪

The Vow to Vowel

As we're thinking, silently talking to ourselves, there's a continual stream of ideas that we identify with our inner self. Even in prayer and contemplative practices, the brain is creating the play of life, and to think and feel without words can lead us to an awakening that's rich with reward.

Donna was a mother of four children. She delighted in playing when her children were small, but found that as they grew, she was more and more withdrawn. Many years ago she attended an evening lecture I gave on the voice and the ear. After a simple three-minute exercise on the soft humming sound, I could see her crying. A barrier had been broken, and there was no place to put her thoughts. The energy was flowing.

Not wanting to turn our evening into a therapeutic session, I suggested that we begin to experiment and play with our voices with our eyes closed. I told the group that we should close our eyes and begin to tell stories of one of the happiest times of life, using only vowels. The energy of the room changed immediately with *cooous, ouuus,* and *aaahhs;* there were swaying and rocking movements. Donna seemed to be petting an imaginary cat or puppy while singing.

A few weeks later I received a call from her saying that years of depression had suddenly subsided. Her toning voice had been able to find the joy she'd experienced with her small children. Her therapist had only asked her to talk about it, but now she was able to sound out her sadness, implant joy, and integrate her thoughts with her feelings. She said that she'd "vow to vowel" every day with consciousness and awareness in order to release tension and fear, renewing balance and energy in her life.

Your experiments with voice and sound may not be as dramatic as Donna's, but they can add a remarkable tool for daily balance. In your car, in the shower, during meditation, while exercising, or at work, take a moment and tone your mind. The more you practice for short periods of time, the more likely you are to acquire the necessary vocabulary for being able to "think the sound" in times of pain, depression, or challenge. It's so simple and so effective. Just take the vow to vowel.

Using Voice, Music, Visualization, and Affirmations for This Chapter

Step One

Take three or four minutes to sit comfortably, release your breath, and imagine blowing out a candle with the sound of *OOUU.*

Affirmation:
OOUU . . . beauty refreshes and renews.

Take a few minutes to feel the affirmation . . . then close your eyes and whisper it to yourself . . . then think it silently.

Step Two

After the affirmation feels comfortable and spontaneous, look at the design on page 81. This stable and concrete portal holds a simple white oval in its center.

- Look at it for a few minutes without blinking. Sit up with the book directly in front of you so that your head isn't tilting down.

- Notice your breath and how the energy in the design may change during your slow breathing.

- Now begin to *oouu* as you gaze into this form.

- Then add the affirmation for a few minutes: *OOUU . . . beauty refreshes and renews.*

- Close your eyes, gently sit in quiet, and feel the effects of the exercise.

Step Three

Track 4 is unique. It is based on the charming text by Jane Taylor about the seasons of life of the small cuckoo bird. Here the *oouu* sound is apparent and sings in clear concert with the music.

Cuckoo, Cuckoo.
What do you do?
In April I open my bill;
In May I sing night and day;
In June I change my tune;
In July far-far I fly;
In August away I must.

Play Track 4 of the enclosed CD, "Cuckoo!" (from "Friday Afternoons," Op. 7, No. 3), by Benjamin Britten.

- Look at the figure, and envision entering the oval.

- Begin the music.

- Think the *OOUU* sound, feeling its energy as you look and listen.

- When Track 4 finishes, turn off the CD and sit with your eyes closed. Notice your inner sense of balance.

♪

OOUU . . .
beauty refreshes and renews.

Music: Track 4,
Benjamin Britten, "Cuckoo!" (from "Friday Afternoons"
Op. 7, No. 3) Alexander Wells, piano; Skaila Kanga, harp;
New London Children's Choir, Ronald Corp, conductor; 1:39

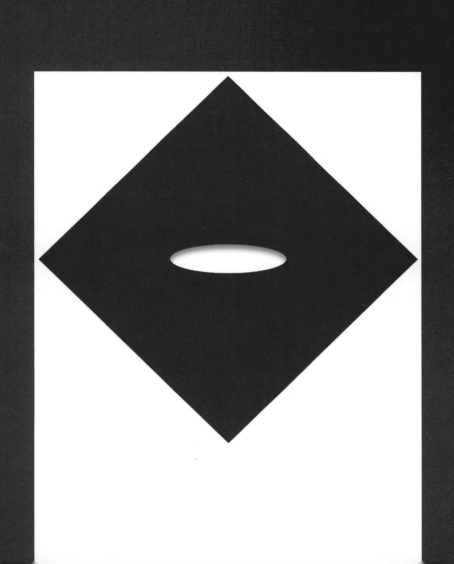

What I observe about my breath:

_____

_____

_____

_____

_____

What I feel from the music:

_____

_____

_____

_____

_____

What I notice with the *OOUU* sound:

_____

_____

_____

_____

_____

What I sense from the image with tone:

_____

_____

_____

_____

_____

Music is the answer to the mystery of life;

It is the most profound of all the arts;

It expresses the deepest thoughts of life and being

In simple language which nonetheless

Cannot be translated.

♦♦♦ ARTHUR SCHOPENHAUER ♦♦♦

Chapter 5

The Healing Moment

*H*ealing is an everlasting process, and life flows with the rhythms of tension and release. From the blood to the breath, these automatic impulses for life are essential for the stimulation of the mind and the moods. Healing is a place where we balance the inner workings and the outer experience of life.

Just as fine music can't quite be completely still, neither can the muscles stay healthy by just being in a passive, relaxed state. During the stress of each day, soft and slow sounds may help us maintain a sense of calm and peace, yet without variations in movement and thought, we become so passive that the sense of being alive and awake passes unnoticed.

The healing moment isn't only the elimination of pain and stress, but also the time of breakthrough and integration. At times it is peaceful and transformational, while at others it is dynamic, forceful, and filled with release.

Music holds the powers of tension and release in its harmony, pace, and structure. *Great* music delivers a message not only to the mind but also to the deepest parts of the spirit. Operas, musicals, and tone poems all bring attention to the episodes of birth, celebration, death, and drama in the style of the time. The search for the lost chord is ever present in our will to be fulfilled.

The sonic clutter around us, however, creates tension in the mind. We have to ignore and eliminate the constant stimulation of unwanted noise. Some forms of ambient music, a passive New Age style, disregard the outer environment and create safe rooms for our spirit and body. At times this creates a type of bottled mood, a sonic pill. By repetitive and elongated tones and harmonies, this type of music seeks to effect a psychological change by creating an imaginary landscape.

The impressionist map of New Age music ranges from the simplest of flutes singing the joy of a sunrise to the most overwhelming electronic color spectrum where one is swimming in ultraviolet tones; the holy minimalism of Arvo Pärt elongates Gregorian chant to expansive proportions. All of these styles are all saying, "Slow down, listen, and just be."

Music today helps us live in a variety of places simultaneously. Just a quick browse through commercial radio will take you everywhere from gospel music to as many as 15 styles of rock. Living on the lower bands of FM, you may find the warm moments of classical music and the explorations of sonic sweetness during the *Hearts of Space* radio program. (It is amazing to me that "public" radio doesn't appeal to a great portion of the public.)

Our culture searches for the entertaining moment in media. Perhaps we also have to make an effort to find the alternative, creative, and healing moment that dwells in the iPod, church, concert hall, and therapist's office. It lives at times in film music and in nature. Notice how loud beauty can be in silence; and seek the music that's like perfume, seducing you to breathe deeply and know that peace and true refreshment are near.

Deeper Listening

In designing this book, I wanted to provide a number of ways to enter into sound. Using the powerful images with varied shapes like peepholes in the middle helps focus listening and concentration. Just looking at the shapes for a long period of time and then closing the eyes allows the mind to rest. Finding music that would stand alone as a beauteous snack, inspiring and refined, was essential. Yet you can also listen to the whole CD a number of times and flow with the many different textures and moods. Integrating the simple vowel sounds with the visual and auditory elements gives your mind ample ways to settle down into patterns.

Still, nothing can be more important than knowing that you have an inner voice that goes with you to work and also to bed at night. While walking through our valleys and shadows of challenge, we do know that the voice of comfort is with us, not speaking, but holding us in resonance and tone.

Pauline Oliveros is a great pioneer in the musical and spiritual art of listening. She doesn't limit her definition of music to the sounds that are organized by composers. As a creator, she maintains a remarkable balance of:

1. All the music she has ever heard

2. All the sounds of the natural world she has ever heard, including her own biological sounds

3. All the sounds of the technological world she has ever heard

4. All the sounds from her imagination

How to use this immense palette of sound is described in her remarkable book, *Software for People* (Smith Publications, Baltimore, 1984): "My music is the result of the processing of these materials by my own attention and perceptual organization in interaction with traditional ways or models, as well as with new ways made possible by technology." The creative power of her work and teaching in the past decades imprints many generations of composers.

In a Zen-like manner, Pauline Oliveros suggests that we practice listening just as we would a sport. In her lecture "Sonic Images," she asks 17 questions such as: "Can you find a quiet place in your mind where there are no thoughts, no words, and no images?" Most of us would respond with some kind of negative answer. Is it a trick question? How can one be awake and truly not think? Wouldn't it be some phase of sleep or stupor?

In my own meditative and contemplative practices, I think that this has been the greatest of all challenges. Whether using the Centering Prayer or long periods of sitting meditation, I could never quite find that pure, still place where my mind wasn't observing and judging my success at not thinking.

It was during my first experiences of toning that I was able to use the power of sound to sweep away that endless conversation of inner thought. The experiments with the vowel sounds allowed me a quick and simple path to this clear mind. I've toned in every conceivable situation: for eight hours on a plane to South Africa, in a long line at the grocery store, in my dreams, while driving along the California coast, in the dentist's chair, during lovemaking, and even as I've watched concerts.

When I've been off center and out of tune with my heart, I've been able to tone myself back to balance. It's a magnificent healing tool—both loud and silent, filled with every emotion. It can clean out my thoughts and awaken new ones. Tone automatically aligns the body and puts my breath in order.

It's a stimulant, pacifier, and rugged taskmaster. How I want to go into a chant or song to entertain my own mind and body! Tone continually cleanses me and clears me. It's a laxative of sorts for my pent-up feelings, as well as a trigger for creativity and discipline. Pardon the pun, but tone is truly a "vowel movement."

"The Voice Produces Only What the Ear Can Hear"

Dr. Alfred Tomatis challenged the medical, educational, and musical world with that statement. When I met him in the 1980s, I had already started toning. With his "electronic ear," he could modify the way my voice sounded; and by using bone conduction, he could change its richness and color. While wearing headphones and using a microphone to stimulate my ears with my own voice, he could shift my ability to sing in or out of tune. It contradicted everything I'd been taught.

I realized that I'd never been taught about the ear's ability to listen; I only understood the basic mechanism. When he amplified specific ranges in my left ear, I actually lost track of my vocal control and felt like I was a total non-singer. Then he switched the frequencies to the right ear, and suddenly I was in tune with myself again.

While serving as director of the Institute of Music, Health, and Education, I formally tested more than 500 students with right- and left-ear stimulation and observed how the texture and tuning of their voices changed. By looking at their audiological listening charts, there was often an obvious way to see if the students' ears were hypersensitive to certain parts of their vocal ranges. It was in those places that the ability to sing in tune was challenged. Often, there'd be a place where tone perception in one of the ears was weak—and it always showed up in the voice.

Dr. Tomatis told me the story of the melancholy monks at a Benedictine abbey in the south of France. He was called there a few years after Vatican II because they were experiencing stress, fatigue, and sleep disorders. The abbot thought that there was some kind of virus slowly killing the monks. After many specialists had examined the men, only Tomatis realized that they'd been slowly weaned off their routine of singing Gregorian chant nine times a day. This had been replaced with only a few services sung in French in a new style.

The despondence of the monks wasn't physiological, but audiological! Tomatis put the monks back on a full diet of chant. Within weeks, the elongated tones of devotional praise and prayer had restored the health of the abbey residents.

Most of the doctor's writings and work deal with speech, language, and communications. In hundreds of centers worldwide, children with ADD and ADHD are able to retrain their listening and auditory skills. Autistic children often benefit from his methods, also.

Slowly, with the research and development of his basic concepts, these Copernican ideas are changing the way we think about music, sound, and health.

Now Is the Moment

It's been more than 18 years since I wrote *The Roar of Silence,* my earlier work on toning and the voice; and in the process of writing this book, it's been such a delight to rethink the thousands of experiences I've had in workshops and classes with tone. Stories about instant healing always stunned me, yet I believe that the miracle was just ready to happen. Stories about obsessive-compulsive toning also floored me, with people telling me that nothing ever seemed to happen and no experience was enough. No matter what their reactions, my role was always to bring students to the center, the place of balance.

Tone is practical, neither weird nor esoteric. It's just good, healthy, homegrown vibration. It need not be either haunting or mystical, instead being basic and fundamental. It serves as a foundation for language, emotions, music, and energy.

It's my sincerest wish that the beauty of the music on the CD, the forms of the images, and the power of the vowels will bring you to a creative and resource-ful place of balance and wellness. Join me for times of resonance and refreshment every day. May your world in every corner sing and tone!

Using Voice, Music, Visualization, and Affirmations for This Chapter

Step One

Take three or four minutes to sit comfortably, re-lease your breath, and imagine light and sound radi-ating throughout the body with the sound of *oooo.*

Affirmation:
OOOO . . . the wonder of sound.

Take a few minutes to feel the affirmation . . . then close your eyes and whisper it to yourself . . . then think it silently.

Step Two

After the affirmation feels comfortable and spontaneous, look at the design on page 101. This stable and concrete portal holds a simple white circle in its center.

- Look at it for a few minutes without blinking. Sit up with the book directly in front of you so that your head isn't tilting down.

- Notice your breath and how the energy in the design may change during your slow inhalations and exhalations.

- Now begin to make the *oooo* sound as you gaze into this round form. You may wish to make this sound as an "om" in the Eastern tradition or as an "Oh!" of surprise before you settle into the pure sound.

- Then add the affirmation for a few minutes: *OOOO . . . the wonder of sound.*

- Close your eyes, gently sit in quiet, and feel the effects of the exercise.

Step Three

Play Track 5 of the enclosed CD. Rachmaninoff originally wrote this eloquent piece called "Vocalise" for voice and piano. Here, it's played on the cello. Pensive and haunting, it's a perfect piece of music to sense the fullness of the *oooo* sound.

- Look at the figure, entering into the circle.

- Begin the music.

- Think the *oooo* sound, feeling its energy as you look and listen.

- When Track 5 finishes, turn off the CD and sit with your eyes closed. Notice the inner sense of balance.

♪

OOOO . . .
the wonder of sound.

Music: Track 5
Rachmaninoff, "Vocalise," Op. 34, No. 14; Maria Kliegel, cello;
Raymund Havenith, piano; 6:53

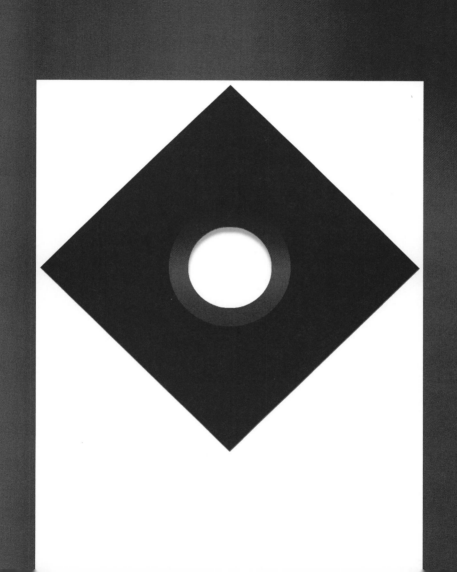

What I observe about my breath:

_____

_____

_____

_____

_____

What I feel from the music:

_____

_____

_____

_____

_____

What I notice with the *OOOO* sound:

_____

_____

_____

_____

_____

What I sense from the image with tone:

_____

_____

_____

_____

_____

CD Track List

1. J. S. Bach, "Piano Concerto No. 5 in E Major, BWV 1056 - Largo," Hae-won Chang, piano; Camerata Cassovia, Róbert Stankovsky, conductor; 2:46

2. Satie, "Gymnopédie No. I," Gerald Garcia, guitar; CSFR State Philharmonic Orchestra (Kosice), Peter Breiner, conductor; 2:59

3. Rachmaninoff, "Eighteenth Variation," (from "Rhapsody on a Theme by Paganini," Op. 43, arranged by F. Kreisler), Takako Nishizaki, violin; Jenö Jandó, piano; 2:55

4. Benjamin Britten, "Cuckoo!" (from "Friday Afternoons," Op. 7, No. 3) Alexander Wells, piano; Skaila Kanga, harp; New London Children's Choir, Ronald Corp, conductor; 1:39

5. Rachmaninoff, "Vocalise," Op. 34, No. 14, Maria Kliegel, cello; Raymund Havenith, piano; 6:53

Suggested Reading

Cymatics. Hans Jenny. Newmarket, NH: Macromedia, 2001.

Expanding Tonal Awareness. Heiner Ruland, translated by John F. Logan. London: Rudolf Steiner Press, 1992.

The Healing Power of the Human Voice: Mantras, Chants, and Seed Sounds for Health and Harmony. James D'Angelo. Rochester, VT: Healing Arts Press, 2000.

Healing Sounds: The Power of Harmonics. Jonathan Goldman. Rockport, MA: Element, Inc., 1992.

The Healing Voice. Paul Newham. Boston, MA: Element, Inc., 1999.

The Roar of Silence. Don Campbell. Wheaton, IL: Quest Books, 1989.

Set Your Voice Free. Roger Love with Donna Frazier. Boston, New York, London: Little, Brown, 1999.

The Sonic Thread, Sound as a Pathway to Spirituality. Cynthia Snodgrass. New York: Paraview Press, 2002.

Toning: The Creative Power of the Voice. Laurel Elizabeth Keyes. DeVorss and Company, 1964.

The Vocal Vision: Views on Voice by 24 Leading Teachers, Coaches & Directors. Edited by Marion Hampton and Barbara Acker. New York: Applause, 1997.

Who Is Singing? Embracing the Physical and Spiritual Dimension of the Voice. Silvia Nakkach. Available in 2008.

♪

For more information on Don Campbell's books and CDs; as well as a vast guide to music, music therapy, education, and health:

The Mozart Effect Resource Center
P. O. Box 800
Boulder, CO 80306
800-721-2177
www.mozarteffect.com

For more information on schools of voice and healing, contact:

Open Ear Center, Inc., Pat Cook, Director
P. O. Box 10276
Bainbridge Island, WA 98110
206-842-5560
www.openearcenter.com

The Vox Mundi Project, Silvia Nakkach, Director
The Besler Building
4053 Harlan St. #202- Loft # 202
Emeryville, CA 94608
510-595-0819
www.voxmundiproject.com

Suggested Listening

Deep Listening. Pauline Oliveros. New Albion Records NA022 (background music for toning)

Thursday Afternoon. Brian Eno. EG, Opal, Jem Records (background music for toning)

♪

Healing Powers of Tone and Chant. Don Campbell. Quest Books (instructional)

Healing Sounds. Jonathan Goldman. Spirit Music 27007 (instructional)

Healing Yourself with Your Own Voice. Don Campbell. Sounds True W105D (instructional)

Heal Yourself with Sound & Music. Don Campbell. Sounds True W2477D (instructional)

The Roar of Silence. Don Campbell. Quest Audio (instructional)

The Wisdom and Power of Music. Don Campbell. Quest Audio (instructional)

Acknowledgments

My deepest appreciation goes to Bill Horwedel at Spring Hill Music for his visionary practicality and friendship. Thanks to Reid Tracy, Jill Kramer, Jessica Vermooten, Christy Salinas, and Charles McStravick at Hay House for their skillful development of this book.

My sincere gratitude to Marianne Cenko for her artistic insight, editing, and proofing. Thanks also to Jeanne Achterberg, Cassandra Volpe, and Julia Cameron.

About the Author

Don Campbell is a recognized authority on the transformative power of music, listening, and The Mozart Effect®. He's a leading lecturer and consultant to health-care organizations, corporations, parenting groups, and schools. He works with audiences of symphony orchestras on how music can affect learning, healing, and other aspects of our lives.

Don is the acoustic and musical director of Aesthetic Audio Systems, an innovative company that provides quality music to health-care facilities. His books have been translated into 20 languages; and he has lectured in more than 25 countries, including South Africa, Brazil, Poland, Ireland, India, Israel, and Japan. He has recently keynoted conferences for Yale University, the Royal Dublin Society, the Society for the Arts in Healthcare, and the International Teachers Associations in Japan and South America. He presently serves on the board of the American Music Research Center at the University of Colorado.

Don serves on many national boards, including ARTS for People and the Duke University Medical School. In 2004, he was honored with the Distinguished Fellow award from the National Expressive Therapy Association. He has also been awarded "Director Emeritus" of the Boulder Philharmonic Orchestra. In Don's unique view, music is not only a rich and rewarding aesthetic experience, but an easily accessible bridge to a more creative, intelligent, healthy, and joy-filled life. His singular mission is to help return music to its central place in the modern world as a resource for growth, development, health, and celebration.

Don is the author of 18 books, including *Music: Physician for Times to Come*, *Rhythms of Learning*, and the 1997 bestseller *The Mozart Effect*. He has also produced 16 albums, including the accompanying music for the Mozart Effect series for adults and children, which dominated the classical *Billboard* charts in 1998 and 1999.

Notes

Notes

Notes

Notes

Notes

Notes

Notes

Notes

Notes

Hay House Titles of Related Interest

Books

Angel Medicine: *How to Heal the Body and Mind with the Help of the Angels,* by Doreen Virtue, Ph.D.

Getting in the Gap: *Making Conscious Contact with God Through Meditation,* by Dr. Wayne W. Dyer

Heal Your Body, by Louise L. Hay

Inner Peace for Busy People, by Joan Z. Borysenko, Ph.D.

Silent Power, by Stuart Wilde (book-with-CD)

Sound Choices: *Using Music to Design the Environments in Which You Live, Work, and Heal,* by Susan Mazer and Dallas Smith

CDs

The Beginner's Guide to Meditation, by Joan Z. Borysenko, Ph.D.

Complete Relaxation, by Denise Linn

The Divine Name: *Sounds of the God Code,* by Gregg Braden and Jonathan Goldman

All of the above are available at your local bookstore, or may be ordered by contacting Hay House (see next page).

♪

We hope you enjoyed this Hay House book.
If you'd like to receive a free catalog featuring additional
Hay House books and products, or if you'd like information about the
Hay Foundation, please contact:

Hay House, Inc.
P.O. Box 5100
Carlsbad, CA 92018-5100

(760) 431-7695 or **(800) 654-5126**
(760) 431-6948 (fax) or **(800) 650-5115 (fax)**
www.hayhouse.com® • **www.hayfoundation.org**

Published and distributed in Australia by: Hay House Australia Pty. Ltd.,
18/36 Ralph St., Alexandria NSW 2015 • *Phone:* 612-9669-4299
Fax: 612-9669-4144 • www.hayhouse.com.au

Published and distributed in the United Kingdom by: Hay House UK,
Ltd., 292B Kensal Rd., London W10 5BE • *Phone:* 44-20-8962-1230
Fax: 44-20-8962-1239 • www.hayhouse.co.uk

Published and distributed in the Republic of South Africa by:
Hay House SA (Pty), Ltd., P.O. Box 990, Witkoppen 2068
Phone/Fax: 27-11-706-6612 • orders@psdprom.co.za

Published in India by: Hay House Publishers India, Muskaan Complex,
Plot No. 3, B-2, Vasant Kunj, New Delhi 110 070 • *Phone:* 91-11-4176-1620
Fax: 91-11-4176-1630 • www.hayhouse.co.in

Distributed in Canada by: Raincoast, 9050 Shaughnessy St.,
Vancouver, B.C. V6P 6E5 • *Phone:* (604) 323-7100
Fax: (604) 323-2600 • www.raincoast.com

Tune in to **HayHouseRadio.com®** for the best in inspirational talk radio featuring
top Hay House authors! And, sign up via the Hay House USA Website to receive the
Hay House online newsletter and stay informed about what's going on with your
favorite authors. You'll receive bimonthly announcements about: Discounts and
Offers, Special Events, Product Highlights, Free Excerpts, Giveaways, and more!
www.hayhouse.com®